Breaking and Mending

Anna Gray

BookLeaf Publishing

Presentation by *BookLeaf Publishing*

Web: www.bookleafpub.com

E-mail: info@bookleafpub.com

ISBN: 9789357445269

First edition 2021

DEDICATION

To all my wonderful family and friends who have supported me on my journey. My parents and sister who have taken me to endless appointments, fought for what is best for me and always been at the end of the phone - I couldn't ask for a better bunch of people to be on my team!

Chronic

Imagine your days spent bedbound
Shackled to the sheets, unable to move
Every twist and turn of your body
Sending searing pain from head to toe
Or moving from the bed to the sofa and calling it quits
Knowing that your day will be spent
Half watching the crap daytime TV and quiz shows
Or be spent on the bathroom floor,
The wave of nausea overtaking you as you retch and gag
And then lying back, the cold hard floor touching your skin
But being unable to move
Before the next wave comes and knocks you back
Imagine your days spent clock watching
Waiting for the next dose of pain meds to keep it all at bay
Or keeping hot water bottles on rotation so they barely become cool
Before switching it for the next, boiling water fresh from the kettle
TENS machine permanently attached

The endless nights that drag on for what feels like years
When in reality only moments have passed
Pain rushing through you and yet no matter the position you lie,
You're uncomfortable
Writhing in discomfort under the duvet, shifting and twisting and turning
Wishing that the hours would pass until the alarm signals its ok to take meds
The phone calls to doctors that seem to happen on repeat
Receptionists who must remember your name,
Recognise your number, recall all your details
As you try to explain to yet another GP that you need their help
You need more PRN or more advice, more management plans or tests
Dropping off samples becoming a regular thing
Dragging yourself down to the surgery to get it in on time
Before the wait to find out what will help – has the gamble on antibiotics paid off?
Or will it all be in vain? Will you get another call for another script?
Your energy being expended on yet another trip down
Rather than being able to save it for another day
Trying to stay inside and build up some spoons

Imagine a life turned upside down by this
Unwelcome visitor keeping you trapped a
prisoner in your own home
Imagine being held hostage inside your own
body
Outwardly appearing ok and fine and holding it
together
Inside a prisoner, a prisoner to the bed or the
sofa or the bathroom floor or hospital ward
Hoping and praying that maybe one day it'll all
go away
But secretly being aware that it's hear to stay
Never ending, everlasting, a recurring pain,
A nightmare, ceaseless, incessant, unwelcome
guest
The chronic illness here to stay, detaining you to
the same four walls
Like some pawn in a sick, twisted game of chess

But you don't look sick

You don’t look sick, they say
As if you should wear it like a badge of honour
A medal weighing heavy on your chest
You don’t look sick, are you sure it’s real?
Are you sure it’s not just a figment of your imagination,
Your head running wild on an adventure?
You don’t look sick, so why can’t you come
Out on a trip or do certain things?
As if sickness is defined by a look,
As if you’re only sick if you can’t walk or talk or eat
Like a ‘normal’ person can
But what even is ‘normal’?
The one work we banned in psychology class
The swear word that was forbidden to leave our lips
Yet we wish we were ‘normal’ or could do ‘normal’ things,
Yearn for it and pine after some sense of normality.
You don’t look sick, maybe you’re just lazy?

As if that thought has never run rampant through your brain before
As if you've not spent many a night sat up, feeling like a fraud
And wondering if in some twisted way you've made it all up,
Or are doing something wrong
Like a switch that needs to be turned on or a computer that needs to be restarted
You don't look sick, they say,
As if it's as simple as 'have you tried turning it off and back on again'?
Like you should be able to restart your body in some way
So you have more functionality, or provide some sort of update
When I hear the words 'you don't look sick'
I somehow start wishing that I hurt in a more obvious way

The Waiting Room

You walk into the waiting room
And immediately are the anomaly
People look up, confusion painted on their faces
Surely you can't be in this clinic?
You must have done to the wrong department
You're far too young to be sitting in here
Always an anomaly to the situation
Reassuring and sympathetic smiles from fellow patients
The puzzled checking of appointment letters
As if chronic illness can't affect young people
As if bladders are reliable for all
Or start to dysfunction once you reach middle aged
A urology nurse once said to me
'I really wish we had a young poster girl,
Someone young to go on the leaflets because then
People would know they're not on their own'
And it's true
Every leaflet I've ever picked up in a hospital waiting room
Has shown older people in hospital transport,
Or sitting waiting for tests,

Or speaking to the consultant and getting news, both good and bad
But it has never been someone like me, never a young man or young woman
Never a teenager or a young adult on the glossy front covers
Saying 'hey this waiting room is a space for all'
Chronic illness sucks for everyone, I get that, I do
But it especially sucks when you're the opposite of the preconceived idea of a chronically ill person
When even the doctors don't know what to say or do
Because the situation is so fragile, so complex that they don't want to disrupt the balance
So you get left floating in limbo, living a half life
Living in the murky grey – you're not drowning but you're not swimming either
You're kind of floating along, waiting for the lifeboat
To pull you to safety, to some sort of plan
And when you leave the appointment
You know you have to face to waiting room again
With the stares and looks of confusion and pity
Painted on faces yet again
Knowing that this cycle is your life now.

Imagine

Imagine waking up every day,
Being more tired than the night before
The few hours sleep you managed to grab
Not alleviating your exhaustion at all
Imagine changing your outfit twenty times in one morning
Nothing looking right with the catheter
The bag looking too obvious, the site being rubbed
Irritation and pain making moving impossible
Imagine not wanting to see anyone at all
Because you're ashamed of what your health has done to you
Or trying to make plans
But needing to plan everything around the nearest public loo
And packing spare clothes and equipment 'just in case'
Imagine the constant pain
A stabbing, burning, searing, crippling pain
Keeping you confined to the bed or the sofa or the floor
Moving exacerbating it all, causing it to fill every inch of brain space

Imagine being told everything is 'all in your head'
Doctors sceptical that any of this is even real
Shrinks being sent to see you – 'how is your mental health these days?'
Thinking you're lying because you're 'too young'
(Because of course all of this is being done for a laugh,
Like we can't think of things we would rather do)
Or being asked 'what do you want us to do?'
With no forward plan or relief or comfort
Being left alone to try manage as best you can
Imagine being on antibiotics day after day
Infection intensifying the pain and symptoms
Yet never fully going away
Never being sure if the nausea and sickness
Is because of your meds or because you're unwell
Imagine spending your days spending hours and hours
Trawling the internet for answers
For experimental treatments and surgery and private opinions
Weighing up the pros and cons of spending your savings
On a private consultation to try avoid the long wait,

Or trying to get someone to listen and take you seriously
Imagine not working because the effects take over your life
Physically and mentally unable to deal with the demands
Working life places on your body, it being too much to bare
Imagine being told that major surgery is on the cards
Something you hoped, prayed, wished would be light years away
Living your life in and out of hospital
If you can truly call that 'living'
Imagine your body not feeling like it belongs to you
Instead, feeling like it belongs to the countless professionals
Who don't have the answers
Or the understanding of how painful and traumatic
The repeated trips are, not seeing the panic attacks
And anxiety building up when you're on your own
Imagine losing a vital body function literally overnight
No warning, no signs, BAM! - it hits
Flipping your life on its head, leaving you lost

A bladder that hates you, is determined to cause pain
The new routines becoming a staple part of your day
Boxes of medical equipment and prescription meds
Building up in your home
So no matter where you look you can't escape
The loss of your 'normal' everyday life.

- Fowler's fighters: you are brave, you are strong, you've got this!

They say ignorance is bliss

Have you tried yoga?
Or mindfulness or a bath?
Acupuncture or herbal remedies,
I had a friend once, drank only green tea
For weeks on end and it cured her pain
Maybe you could try it?
Endless detoxes or pills suggested
Maybe if you just thought positive
The pain would go away?

- And maybe if I punched you, your ignorance would just go away?

Left Out

It's hard not to feel left out
When wherever you look, left, right and centre
You see pictures of friends
Graduating uni, getting dream jobs
Marrying or announcing pregnancies or births
It's hard not to feel left out
When it feels like everyone in the world
Well, everyone except you
Seems to be moving on with their life
Whilst you're stuck behind,
Frozen in time, trapped in the ice
Unable to progress at the speed of your peers
Feeling jealous of their accomplishments
But also unbelievably proud and happy
That they're getting the life they deserve
It's hard not to feel left out
When your memories pop up on facebook,
snapchat or timehop
And you remember the things you were able to
do
Five, ten, fifteen years ago
That are no longer possible or feasible now
It's hard not to feel left out
When you have to turn down invites from
friends

Painfully aware that one day the invites will
probably just stop
An automatic assumption that you'll just say no
People being oblivious to how much this might
hurt
Oblivious to just how much even being asked
means
It's hard not to feel left out
When you spend most of your days staring at the
same four walls
Re-watching the same films and programmes on
repeat
Listening to the same music and reading the
same books
Clock watching until it's time for meds
It's easy to feel left out
Easy because you want it so badly
Internally begging to be included or thought of
And when it doesn't always happen
Feeling left out becomes the easiest thing in the
world

Guilt

Having a chronic illness is like being handed a fastpass to guilt
It's good at that – good at guilty feelings
That gnaw away at us, reminding us of what we cannot do
Nagging thoughts that we are 'not good enough'
Or that we 'can't do enough' or that we 'are a burden'
Guilt overtaking our mind
Clouding judgement and every thought
Becomes tainted with the inadequacy that guilt lavishes on us
Deep down we might know that
None of this is our fault
We didn't wake up one morning and go
'Oh, you know what sounds good? Chronic illness'
But in the moment it's so hard to take on board
Chipping away, wearing us down
Guilt heavy on our backs and shoulders
The ableism that runs rampant in society today
Twists peoples minds so they believe
That asking for help is a drain on others
Like a neon sign in the dark flashing bright
A message of 'you're not worthy of this'

Flashing bright so everyone can see
Hanging over you or like a shadow following your every move
Rationalising can help us to see
See that it isn't our fault, no one asks to be ill
We want to join in, don't want to miss out
On the plans we had sorted with friends
Yet we feel guilt over plans being changed
For it is not a choice or out of spite
Yet deep down we feel guilt
Guilt because maybe if it wasn't for us
Things would have gone ahead
Guilt for being unwell, for something so out of our control
And a deep sadness inside
Wishing that we could just get on with life in the normal way

A New Kind of Grief

I never fully understood
What it meant to grieve, what it ever felt like
To be in that place of darkness and sorrow and pain
Until I had to start grieving for my body
I didn't even know it was possible to grieve for your body,
To grieve when no one has passed

Instead I'm grieving for the lost opportunities,
The hours spent in appointments that I'll never get back
The bodily functions that I've lost forever
Grieving for the body I had pre-chronic illness
And the things I could do with it
I knew it would be hard, just not this hard
Grieving for a life I dreamt of or the 5 year plan
I had mapped in my head

But people say grief gets easier over time
That the pain lessens and it hurts less and less each day

I haven’t quite felt that yet,
But maybe it’s the hope I need to hold on to.

- things won’t always feel this way darling

Psychiatric Ward

The door slams shut, there's the jangle of keys
With a twist of the lock, the world shut out behind you
A place to house the mentally ill, to keep them safe
The sterile, suicide-proof rooms that are blank and bare
Beds bolted to the floor and heavily weighted chairs
The curtains stuck up with magnets, so they fall if you pull
And doors that open both in and out
So you can't escape from the staff, can't hide away from them all
So they can access your room even if you try to barricade
Yourself away from the rest of the ward
There's sometimes a bathroom, with a crappy sink and shower
That turn off after seconds, not minutes, with no plugs or mirrors
There are plastic mugs and plates and knives
And hospital food, if you can even call it food, the sludge on a plate
Three times a day for as long as your there

Or the sandwiches that taste of cardboard with a hint of butter
People often ask, 'what is it like, being shut away in there?'
The easy answer is to tell them its like being stuck in hell, no way out
Unfamiliar environment, with unfamiliar faces and sounds
Alarms being pulled to signal distress, staff running across the floor
Shouting at each other to grab the oxygen, or the scissors, or the phone
To call 999 for emergency help.
It's being checked on every 15 minutes, a hatch in the window pulled down
Or the door being opened to make sure you're still alive
The hours dragging on for what feels like days at a time
Stuck inside the bare, sterile, blank prison with only your thoughts for company
Medication given out multiple times a day
Regular or PRN to calm you down when your distress is too high
Restraints and de-escalation and segregation and stripped rooms
Eyesight and arms-length and no dignity at all
The other patients, all unwell in their own way

Like the woman who believes the water is acid,
tries to warn you not to drink
And thinks the food is contaminated, staff trying
to coax her to take even one bite
Or the one who thinks the government is
tracking their every move
Or watching on spy cameras and controlling
their life
Like the man who was so depressed he saw no
way out
And decided to end it, only someone intervened
and bought him here,
A safe, sterile prison away from the world
Where the mentally ill while away their days
under lock and key
And keen observation until the lock twists once
again in the door
The jangle of keys and the door slamming shut
once again
And they are set free, free to fly once again.

Recovery

My legs are a lot bigger than they used to be
But it's okay that they are, that I occupy more space
They're the legs that let me walk,
Run and explore new places
Rather than keeping me chained to a hospital bed,
With no chance for adventures or experiencing new things
Rather than everyone worrying that you might buckle over at any given moment
So it's okay that they're bigger
(Bigger legs means more room for dogs to sit on your lap, right?!)
I spent so long trying to shrink my stomach,
Wishing that the awkward folds would disappear
And that I'd wake up with no fat to look at in the mirror for hours on end
Failing to realise that my squishy tummy protects all my organs
Keeps me stable and out of harms way
And yes it might look different, but that too is okay
Health is always a priority and shrinking my body will never help my health

My arms have also grown, grown into arms that can hold my loved ones
Arms that can play the piano for hours on end
Pick flowers that smell divine and that can adorn my flat, every corner
Filled with the smell of beautiful freshness that makes anyone smile
My face might be more round too, I have more flesh on my cheeks
And I might weigh more than I did a year ago
But what did shrinking my body ever do for me?
What did I achieve?
Hospital admission and health scares and no independence or freedom at all
Which isn't really living at all
Shrinking my body never gave me the peace of mind I hoped to achieve
So I have to hold on and hope that my bigger, more squishy body
Gives me the life I dream of
That I can finally be at peace with myself and my body
Peaceful, calm, content, happy in my skin
- After all, the only home you get is this one, so treat it well

Evil Twin

You become a hollow shell
A shadow of a person
Secretive and sneaky
Obedient to your evil twin
Who arrived with a sly little smile
And promises of a better life
Like any sibling
It's a love hate relationship
One minute you're best friends
Nothing can separate you
The next you're fighting
Evil twin screaming insults
In a way it's abusive
Manipulative and malicious
You're wrapped around its finger
The grip is tight
And you can't let go
You want to and you try to
But then comes the sly little smile and promises again
When you're at breaking point
Wanting to run away
Suddenly your evil twin
Becomes your best friend again
The one person you can rely on

Even though everyone else
Tells you it wants you dead
There it is
Whispering in your ear
The promises again
You're naïve
Blindly following
Despite the feelings
Deep, deep down
That say this isn't right
Because you don't know
What is right
Or what is normal
Anymore
Your evil twin strips you
Of any identity once had
Monotonous
The voice carries on inside your head
Harder and harder to ignore
Telling you you'll be perfect
If you lose just
One pound more
Your evil twin
Smiles with glee
As the scales begin to drop
But you'll never be skinny enough
It'll constantly push you
Right to the edge
Testing your limits

Until there's no coming back
Acting like your friend
Saying you're doing well
And convincing you it's for the best
That you can keep on
Yet the reality is
Your body is slowly dying
Fading away
An empty shell
A shadow
And for what?
Your so-called friend?
With her sly smile
And monotonous voice
She's no friend
She's horrible
Manipulative
Malicious
Your evil twin

Scars

I remember the first time I wore short sleeves
Well, the first time since the self-harming began
I spent house in front of the mirror
Questioning and deliberating over my outfit
What would people thing? Would they stare?
Would they point?
Hours of changing into different outfits
None of them looking quite right
Before resorting back to the first one anyway.

I remember the first time someone pointed and stared
And told me 'people like you shouldn't be allowed out'
What does that even mean, people like me?
The burning of my cheeks, a scarlet red appearing
From beneath my skin, a visible show of the anger within
I choked back tears and turned away
Not realising that they would be the start of many more comments and stares
Of people telling me that I need to censor my body

Or that they find it disgusting and uncomfortable and horrible

I remember the looks of disgust and disgrace
That people have pulled when they look my way
Or the throwaway comments about how it's 'attention seeking'
So people will make a fuss, pay me attention
And no matter how much I have tried to explain
That it is not the case at all, most people don't seem to get it
They don't understand how secretive it is,
How overwhelmingly shameful I feel when they point and stare
Or how I did everything within my power
To keep it hidden as long as I could

It became the start of the summer where I began to feel ashamed
Of what I had done to myself, of the pain I had inflicted upon myself
No one really understanding the deep mental torture
You experience to put yourself through that
I've had scars for 7 summers now,
Most of them faded to white
But I'm still scared every time I leave the house
Scared that people will point and comment and stare

Scared that they'll judge me or make me feel
insane
So I censor my body for their comfort
Shame bubbling away under the surface.

Inner Strength

Recovery is scary
One of the scariest things you'll do
It feels all sorts of things, but it doesn't feel right
And you'll wonder why on earth you're committing to it
After all, it'd be easier to just give in, right?
But one day you'll reach that moment
The moment when you realise that recovery is worth it
That it is worth every tantrum, every tear,
Every argument with your head
Worth the battles you fight
Silently in your mind every night
The battles that no one else sees or knows about
And you start to see what life can truly be about
Life without an eating disorder dictating your every move
Where food can be fun and happy
And a joy to be around
Where one day, it doesn't feel so scary any more
Where life can be full of kindness
It can be productive, hopeful, exciting
You have the strength to get through this
Even though you might not yet believe

But you do – deep within you it's there,
bubbling away
The strength to defy the bully in your mind
The strength to fight against its belittling voice
The strength to keep on, even when you feel you
have no strength left
It is there, within you
And in time you'll come to see
Just how strong you can actually be

Trapped

I walked into the prison cell
Except it didn't look like a cell, didn't feel like a cell
Until I was too long gone, too trapped
Trapped in the suffocating, miniscule space
Desperate to leave but stuck under lock and key
No one around you can see that you're trapped
They shout and scream and plead
Get annoyed and angry and just want you out
Unable to see that you're physically stuck
That you can't just come forward to them
To you it feels impossible
You feel like you have control
Stuck in the safe, familiar dungeon that you call your home
Deep down, somewhere inside, you know you hate it
But even the thought of leaving
Is enough to make you feel sick, nausea overtaking you
'How can I possibly leave this?'
'Maybe I just didn't try hard enough?'
'It's probably better for everyone if I just stay here'
Anorexia becomes your safety blanket,

Keeps you numb from the outside world
Gives you something to focus on, a distraction from life
Picking apart yourself, until there is nothing left to pick
Convinced that you'll never be good enough
Intense loathing searing through your bones
Penetrating every area of your life
Your insecurities impacting your every move
Feeling powerless, motivationless
An impossible situation
Shackled to an invisible cage
A familiar routine that feeling strangely comforting
Unable to set yourself free

This is Me

I have an eating disorder
It's not had, did or used to
It's present tense
Happening now
But things will get better
I am learning
About recovery
And what it is
And what I'll have to do
To get rid of its grip forever
It is learning
Learning to love myself
Learning to let others love me
Surviving when I don't want to
That I deserve to recover
I am trying
Trying to listen to my body
Trying to give myself what I need
Letting others help me
It's about ups and downs and all arounds
I am going slowly
Being patient and gentle
Taking things day by day
Minute by minute
Not being everything to everyone

I'm trying to be accepting
Accepting the words
Anorexia, Anxiety, Depression
But not as a label
Not something to live up to
I am on a journey
It is crying, laughing, all over
Eating is essential
It will be ok though
I will be ok though
It doesn't mean it's easy
But at the moment
This is me

Life Worth Living

A stuffy waiting room, that familiar smell
The smell that only seems to apply to hospitals
A mixture of cleaning products filling the air
Polish and disinfectant, D10 and bleach
Coupled with the uncomfy chairs
That only further act as a sign to your brain that this isn't a place you want to be

When the group starts its another stuffy room
The same uncomfy, lumpy chairs
That look deceptively comfy and soft
Windows locked shut, or open a fraction
But still not enough to circulate fresh air
People sitting in a circle trying to give off the illusion that they want to be there
Even though everyone is aware that they would all
Rather be somewhere else, anywhere else
Yet they turn up anyway – maybe this will be the session
The one that clicks,
The one that starts them on their journey to a life worth living

Each session starts with mindfulness

'Eat the raisin mindfully'
'Explore your inner self'
'Picture your thoughts on leaves,
Floating away down a river, just let them come and go'
Looking up and around you see you're not the only one
Not the only one without an attention span long enough to fully engage
Not the only one who is finding it hard
And trying not to giggle as your eyes make contact
You find your spot on the floor to focus on once more

Bringing your attention back to the room
You get your turn to discuss how it went
Did you find it easy? Or was it too difficult?
'You just need to practice more, ideally twice a day'
'The more you practice the easier it becomes'
The homework sheets come out of bags and make it onto the table
(Although, inevitably a few have 'forgotten'
'Forgotten, or didn't do it, there's a fine line to cross)
And everyone shares examples from their weeks
Situations where the skills were put to good use
Where wise mind made it through

Where they STOPped or TIPPed or DEAR MANned
The hell out of a situation
Urge surfed all night to prevent things from escalating
The other group participants celebrating in their success
And comforting the one who didn't quite remember the skills in time
Everyone reassuring them that it will come
That they can be second nature, automatic reflexes within the mind
That it doesn't make them a failure or a lost cause
Just a struggling human in an overwhelming world

You discuss the skill of the week,
The therapist explaining what it means to use it
Where it might be helpful and how to remember it
Each skill being applied to different situations
And more pieces of paper than a stationary shop stocks,
Each one with prompts and suggestions and analogies
To keep safe in a file for later use,
So your mind can be prompted when you reach the stage

Of such intense emotional distress that things start to bubble over
So you can remember to distract and stay safe
When the waves come crashing, like waves on a beach
On a stormy night, relentless and frequent

You can always try to IMPROVE the moment, or maybe ACCEPTS
Is the way forward, your wise mind guiding the way
Or can you radically accept that the situation is shit
But that you need to ride it out in the hope it can change
PLEASE can you try to reduce your vulnerability,
Be mindful of the emotions before acting in the opposite way
And when it comes to talking to others,
To the interpersonal effectiveness that will help communication
You can try to GIVE FAST and remember the DEAR MAN,
Who can help you stay objective and calm and rational
Your mind becomes a handbook
A handbook for the skills and acronyms and ideas

That can help you make it through
Until you're finally in a place where you can say
'Yes, this is my life worth living'

Climbing Mountains

Recovery, in a way, is like
Climbing a mountain
When you get to the base and look up
At the long journey ahead of you
It can be easy to back out
To say 'I'm not doing that, no way!'
To turn back and leave it for another day
Yet you decide to venture up
You take the first few steps
And decide to carry on up
But the more you go on, the more tired you become
The more you want to pack it all in
To turn back and head down
Because you know what lies at the bottom
And you know the descent is easier
That you could be back at the bottom before you know it
You could go back to comfortable
To the known and familiar
Or you could carry on up, one foot in front of the other
Even though it's unknown, scary, unpredictable
You can take little steps along the narrow
Winding, rocky roads of the mountain

The narrow, winding, rocky roads of recovery
Until you reach the top
Because when you get to the peak of the
mountain
Take in the view around you
Marvel in the beauty of the world
And even though your tired you can appreciate
That the journey was worth it
Worth every minute, every achey bone
Every breath you took was worth it
Because now you can finally say
'I made it'

Inner Spark

They asked me once,
'What does recovery mean to you?'
After all it's so different
Different for different people
Not a one size fits all glove
To be bought in a rush when it's cold
Different things help in different ways
And what helps one
Might not help another
And what recovery is now
Might not be what it is next year
For me, it's fluid
Like water flowing down a stream
But for now recovery means so many things
It's taking things a day at a time
The journey is my own pace
Day by day, step by step
I can only do my best
To get from morning to night
It's accepting where I am in the present
Not being too hard on myself
I'm unwell, have been unwell for a while
And it may take time to heal
But despite that true statement
Recovery is also accepting that

Even though it's not an overnight fix
There are things I can do
Each and every day
Things to make the journey
As bearable as I can
It's about trying to rationalise,
Not letting my thoughts run away with me
Not overthinking or catastrophising
It's about seeing the grey in life
Thing's don't have to be black or white
Good or bad
Things can just 'be'
It's about giving what I can
Not giving my all or giving nothing at all
Accepting that mistakes happen
Because I'm human, fallible,
And there is beauty in the imperfections
Recovery is imperfectly perfect
And that's what makes it mine

Beyond

I used to believe there was nothing beyond my
eating disorder
That life would always revolve around
Counting calories and overexercise
MyFitnessPal and weighing food
Doctors appointments turning into hospital
admissions
Blood pressure machines, blood tests and ECGs
Weekly therapy and weigh ins.
Until I realised that there is so much beyond my
eating disorder
That life with an eating disorder is no life at all
Life cannot be lived to the full
When you're chasing after the impossible
I realised the life I was missing out on
Whilst I was striving to weigh less, striving for
'perfect'
An illusion that never existed
Life with an eating disorder was torture
I want to exercise for fun, eat and be carefree
I never want to give up this life
In fear of weighing even one pound more.

Journey to Self-Acceptance

I'm not the broken girl I used to believe
That I was, who wouldn't achieve
Who always had a negative view
Of herself and her life
Who would never amount to much
Or reach her goals and dreams
So many lessons learned on this journey
To my self-acceptance

I'm a work in progress, fixable
Worthy of restoration
Held together by the kintsugi of my creator
Kintsugi, a friend once told me,
Is used in Japan to fix broken objects
Because they believe that when something
Something once broken
Is mended with gold and has a history
That it becomes more beautiful
And maybe God wants to fix me
Maybe He wants to fix me with gold

I am me and that is enough

I can love myself for who I am
Accepting my flaws and loving myself
Loving myself despite them all
I don't need to turn myself
Into the person I wish I was
Because the person I am
Is enough, it is me

Comparison runs rife in society today
'They're prettier than me',
'They earn more than me'
'I wish I was as clever as…'
It's kind of human nature
To compare ourselves to others
But just as no one else
Can turn into me, I too
Cannot turn into them
No one does a better job of me, than me

It is ok to be a work in progress
I won't get there overnight
'Rome wasn't built in a day, my dear'
Self-acceptance doesn't mean perfection
You can learn from mistakes
Take on board all the lessons
As long as you do the best you can
Self-acceptance isn't a final destination
It's a journey throughout life.

www.ingramcontent.com/pod-product-compliance
Lightning Source LLC
Chambersburg PA
CBHW051739130826
49812CB00033B/922
9789357445269